Steven Berko

AMERICA

Published in Great Britain in 1988 by Hutchinson Ltd,
an imprint of Century Hutchinson Ltd
Brookmount House, 62–65 Chandos Place
Covent Garden, London WC2N 4NW

Century Hutchinson Australia (Pty) Ltd
16–22 Church Street, Hawthorn, Melbourne, Victoria 3122

Century Hutchinson New Zealand Ltd
191 Archers Road, PO Box 40-086, Glenfield, Auckland 10

Century Hutchinson South Africa (Pty) Ltd
PO Box 337, Bergvlei 2012, South Africa

Photoset in Linotron Meridien by
Rowland Phototypesetting Ltd
Bury St Edmunds, Suffolk
Printed and bound in Great Britain by
Anchor Brendon Ltd, Tiptree, Essex

British Library Cataloguing in Publication Data

Berkoff, Steven
  Steven Berkoff's America.
  1. United States. Description & travel
  I. Title
  917.3'04927

ISBN 0-09-172689-1

Steven Berkoff's
AMERICA

☐ ☐ ☐ ☐ ILLUSTRATED BY GRAHAM DEAN ☐ ☐ ☐ ☐

Hutchinson

London Melbourne Auckland Johannesburg

⅃☐Acapulco: Rambo

As I awoke from a wretched slumber, dreaming that I was
dying on stage, the phone spluttered into life. I was to get
on the set immediately! I rushed to my breakfast that was
being laid on my sea-view panoramic balcony and wolfed
down my croissants and coffee whilst eyeing suspiciously
some ragged, grey, wolf-like clouds stealing some thunder
in the distance. The sky had been torn apart from recent
hurricanes and still looked bruised and bloody. I pulled
on the thinnest T-shirt I could find to counter an expected
100°F heat in the Mexican jungle. The air-conditioned cars
sped us to our location. I hadn't worked in a week in this
hurricane-blasted Acapulco and one could sit by the pool
ordering countless margaritas until you were called. For
the stunt men this was like being let out of school and they
swarmed all over the pool, and the available girls, making
lots of noise and discussing overtime. For my part, I
learned scuba diving and even water ski-ing in a local
lagoon which looked like a backdrop for paradise. I was
getting a touch of Montezuma's Revenge, brought about by
an overdose of dodgy fish taco washed down with
Mexicali beer. I wasn't in the mood for work. There was a
lot of hanging around in this one while Stallone and the
director debated the day's shoot and I was reading *The
Conquest of New Spain* by Bernal Diaz. Treacherous
Spanish dogs giving them glass beads in exchange for gold
and conning them with Christianity served with smallpox.
The Kray twins, along with Charlie Richardson, were
jailed for life for doing what the robbers, Cortés, Raleigh
and Cook, were given royal estates for. Thieving and
plunder has to be sanctioned by the state, so throwing all
these thoughts aside and ignoring the lines of begging
hands and wide imploring eyes, we sped down Main
Street, Acapulco, which is a very pleasant street, lined
with great monuments to the gods, like the Acapulco
Plaza Hotel, which is cunningly shaped into an Aztec
'cue' or temple. These vast temples engorge live tourists,
brown them first by the pool, accept their tributes, play
some loud, garish Mexican-American music and spit them
out again after a beer contest and aerobics daily. I had
been growing a tumour of revenge as I stared down at
those porcine bodies in their modest, long swimsuits

shouting and splashing in their hideous daily volleyball in the pool. The only sign of the Mexican revolution was a street we passed called Emiliano Zapata Street . . . or photos of rifle-toting dark figures in huge sombreros that could be bought in the boutique of the hotel.

The set was a tropical POW camp, and I was a Ruskie officer of sorts, flown in to interrogate our unusual captive. The rest of the POWs looked realistically starved and chancrous and it was an eerie sight first thing in the morning . . . our car had sped past the suburbs of Acapulco, past dozens of little stalls mining a small seam of a livelihood selling coconuts and candy. The contrast between the natives and the visitors is appalling, and witnessing babies lying dozing on the laps of begging mothers whose day is earmarked to a piece of pavement, was seeing a sight that the Aztecs had eradicated five hundred years ago before the fag-ends of Europe showed them civilization.

I was by this time sweating buckets, and the heat blast struck me full in the face as I left the air-conditioned taxi. I sped to the little 'honey wagon' or dressing room trailer. It's called 'honey wagon' since it is like a little cell but the only thing you produce in there isn't honey. The Aztecs had little huts along their highways and actually recycled excrement and thought it quite valuable. I was called on to a set swarming with people, including technicians, actors playing Russians, Viets, POWs, plus wardrobe and a hairdresser who seemed to spend her entire life adjusting the way Sly's hair would flop over his forehead after he had been submerged in the slime-pit. When not doing this, there would be a lot of intense talk amongst the make-up and wardrobe about the restaurant the night before. Others were now milling around, including stunt men, stand-ins, extras, and there was Stallone – almost, as he stood on one crooked knee, like a familiar statue in Florence. He was wearing little bikini pants and waiting to be submerged once more in the slime-pit. He was covered with mud, and adorning and sticking to his body was a collection of hand-made leeches. He was lowered into the pit in a kind of leather harness and hung there, waiting to be raised like a piece of cooked meat. And I, svelte, cruel, cunning Ruskie, am about to interrogate him. Movie realism now demands more than Bogart's action in *The African Queen* when he flicked the damned leeches off. No, I take a sharp knife and dextrously slice the nasty slug, leaving behind a red splodge, courtesy of 'props' . . . the heat of the body against the rubber leech ensured the stage blood looked runny and viscous. We did that a few times and then broke for lunch, which was really good, homely Mexican food. We were given T-shirts advertising the movie. It had Sly on the front, muscles bulging and about to pop and veins swimming under the flesh like snakes, while grasping an M60 machine gun as he blasts villains away. It is a marketable formula that he not only gets away with but does well. He co-directs, writes the script and part-produces while at the same time creating a body out of hundreds of mind-numbing and punishing hours in a gym. This regimen makes him a hard taskmaster, and technicians or actors not up to par are flown in and out with the frequency of auditions . . . we are now on our fourth camera man in as many weeks.

Paranoia gets to you and every phone call by the production office had me mentally packing my bags. The heat today blasts over the forest and vast, multicoloured butterflies flicker like kites over the grass, vultures hover above and exquisite dragonflies in gunmetal blue dart over the small stream that runs through our artificial village. We do the take. The sweaty first assistant director, David, an Englishman, is one of the discs of the backbone of England, since although boiling like a beetroot he none the less commands with easy authority a motley assortment of Italians, Greeks and Americans. He is totally unflustered and humorous as if, whilst it is normally beneath his dignity to associate with such scum, he will nevertheless bring us through battle and on to victory. The second assistant, Roy, hardly ever sweats, and I see now that the English inflexibility is their power. They cannot blend, they bring England with them and even if it is 100 degrees outside, inside their minds it is still Pinewood Studios. David doesn't even step into the shade as we all do for a

few seconds. There he is, Captain Hornblower or a great English whale, spouting up great geysers of sweat.

We deposit the multi-million-dollar body once more in the pit and once more I descend from the chopper through lines of 'Russian' soldiers standing to attention as I stride in. The Russian sadist I play is accompanied by a Mongolian giant who keeps claiming that he can fight anyone in the world and that it is unrealistic for Stallone to beat him in the film in a straight fight. I explain that this is movies, but it obviously bothers him a lot. When not preening himself on his martial attributes he hunts down 'pussy' and avails me of all the details of the prior night's conquests. It is a fascinating act as it is accompanied by much gesture and sound effects.

I slide the knife across Sly's stomach again and he pulls back sharply . . . oh, my God! I had made contact with real flesh . . . I prised the horror off and behold, his flesh was intact and firm. He was *acting*! It certainly gave me a scare.

□□□The Town Square, Acapulco, Mexico

Sitting in a warm town square where all the world comes
to mingle at the end of the day, I feel protected as if this
was the town's sanctuary. The stone figures at the end of
the square watch over us, ancient Indian heroes from
Aztec history. The atmosphere is warm and soft and the
square becomes a womb where everybody drifts, and sits
under the large trees or on the stone walls surrounding the
fountains. The big old chestnut trees shelter us and kids
are leaping around the square playing tin whistles and
chasing each other round the fountain. In warm countries
the square is such a haven, a bath of warm human contact
where you can dip your tired spirit. Where in England can
you do this? . . . just to wander in a town square and know
you will be able to merge into the life flow of the people
and be replenished by it. The British have no harbour,
only a dank and foetid pub. But leaving these damp
thoughts aside, let's drift into the perfumed air of the
square.

By some trees in the centre there were shoe-shiners, a
group of men earning a small living, and the smell of their
polish and wax sent a pleasant fragrance through the air.
There were at least five of them and each had an allotted
space, where perhaps for life they would occupy their
little niches. So I had my shoes shined that had run on wet
tar-stained beaches and dusty roads and had never felt the
soft embrace of leather and wax on their dry and frayed
skin. The shoes were stained and the man worked hard to
remove the tar marks and I sat and floated in the gentleness
of the square where thousands have dozed off before me
and I allowed myself to drift in the sensation of fingers
gently patting and stroking my feet. I didn't feel any sense
of his abjectness or my patronage . . . it was just a job and
I was only a pair of feet that had walked for miles that day,
and his hand seemed to restore some life into my concrete-
pounded ends. Poor feet that had thirteen stones crushing
them down into a relentless walk. I sat and tried to compress
all the details into my head; already I was making a verbal
enchillada out of the experience. I didn't even let it cool
and savour it later . . . no, even now I knew I wanted to
write it down, since I was in literature while I was in life.

His shirt had a neat crease, so maybe he had a wife looking after him, and the faces of the men shining shoes had an immense dignity as if accentuated by the task they were doing. Their faces in no way showed any of the ingredients that would condemn them to shining shoes, but rather the reverse. They looked as if they could equally well be doctors or lawyers, which is the patronizing way we have of looking at things, since we come from a land where opportunity has at least some semblance of being democratic. Here where poverty is rife and corruption manifest, an ordinary decent human being could easily end up being a shoe-shine boy for no other reason than his honesty and lack of guile. These people were clean and neatly dressed and looked like they carried their weight and others' in the world.

He was now working at a piece of tar-like substance . . . I felt his hands battling with the elements that had stained my neglected shoes, but he did not give up. Different bottles were being chosen and brought into the struggle, and strong smells drifted up into my nostrils and it smelt like the most fragrant perfume.

The smell and the soothing effect of his hands combined to send me into a tranquil and benevolent mood as I watched the leaves barely tremble on the tree and twilight settle on the square. It was filling up now with after workers and schoolkids and couples sitting silent and holding hands. Old men sat on the fountain's edge and swung their legs. The church bell now sounded the half hour and told the kids how long they had left before rushing home for dinner. The man was finishing off my shoes with a cloth which he unrolled like a bandage and whipped around my heels. He found a resistant stain and searched his cleaning cloth for a relatively under-used piece to apply some more cleaning fluid. He stretched the cloth out and searched the whole of it like you do when trying to find a dry spot on your handkerchief for a runny nose – he did this with great concentration, turning the cloth this way and that. He seemed unable to find a dry or clean patch worthy enough, since my shoes were of a cream-coloured leather and he had to be more careful than usual not to rub some other stain in. Eventually – and this took some time – he found a sufficiently suitable two square inches, wrapped it around two fingers in a swift motion, which made a kind of hard and secure surface, and worked the stain out. It was as if he was looking at the map of the world . . . the cloth. His tenacity impressed me. He seemed totally engrossed, searching and moving it around its four corners, turning it over, and all the while his face expressed nothing but the decision of doing the job to the best of his ability. There was no forced matiness and no humble pie. It was matter of fact. He finished and it was 60 pesos – which today is 30 cents. I gave him 100 pesos which was 50 cents, but that didn't really seem enough. But what was? Only my changing places and doing his shoes would be enough. The poor, or call it the Third World, has been cleaning our shoes for years and it's about time we took our turn . . . When it comes, I hope I shall do it with the same stoicism.

⌐□The Fishermen. Acapulco, Mexico

Watched the nets being drawn in this morning and the boys and men become a fresco of bodies leaning into the shore and moving together one step at a time. They were a reflection of the sea's power and the weight of the net. The net was slowly being drawn in by inches, suggesting some great and bountiful catch when, in fact, the length of rope which dived into the sea and then out to the nets, made the weight considerably heavier; that, and the dragging of the nets across the ocean floor . . . so they leaned on their heels and heaved the slow-moving burden with its mysterious contents being gradually and systematically trapped. The figures pulled against the life in the net, pitting their bodies against the water-soaked ropes that trapped the innocent fish. The ropes were twisted round their shoulders and then entwined around their backs and then pull, pause and step . . . I wanted to take the rope for a while, as if to contribute and make their struggle that bit less; whether this gesture was guilt or just curiosity I didn't know, but they received the gesture with friendly smiles and didn't seem perturbed by this bloated, red-faced tourist wishing to touch and be part of their ritual . . . I became a link in the chain at Acapulco, a chain that stretched back for centuries. After a while the effort became enormous . . . they really were putting all their strength into it. My hands were red and being rubbed raw by the rope. I turned and saw that they had twisted the rope around their bodies, using their bodies as the pivotal force and allowing their body-weight to fall back. I leaned back also, but still had to grip and pull, although with slightly less force than before. So for a while I was pulling my weight, which was no doubt appreciated, since any effort of mine must mean a bit less for them. For the first time I had a clear meaning for the metaphor 'pulling your weight', and how fishermen must trust their colleagues to do so lest they subsidize them with their own precious strength; and how galling it is when your own limited energy is used up the faster because someone is stealing it from you. I wanted to stop. I had made the gesture but now wanted to carry on with my walk and leave them to the pain that was a daily ritual in their lives.

I walked on a while and watched from a distance . . . the net was now almost in, and part of it was being folded as it was dragged up the beach. The contents were still unknown but the dark, slowly diminishing shape held a certain magical excitement, for you could never be sure of the surprises nature might stun us with. Now they were bringing their nets closer and there was a slight movement on the surface of the water as the life within them became inexorably trapped. Small ripples broke the surface and other non-edible life might be trapped in the same net and then die for nothing, but that's the way of life . . . you cast your net and it may trap some undesirable elements. Now there is a crowd of people beginning to form some back-up action by standing behind the nets and preventing the luckier fish which may have leapt out of the net as the water became shallower from escaping. At this point the breakers are pouring over the nets and some of the fish are pouring over the side with them, so these dozen or so men and boys are armed with plastic bags hoping to act as a kind of barrier. The bags are ordinary shopping bags in different colours looking like a kind of fisherman's flag. The men are excited: it seems that what escapes is a kind of bounty, or perhaps it doesn't matter too much since the larger fish will invariably be trapped . . . or perhaps it is a ritual that has been going on for centuries whereby the people get their 'perks' from what they manage to scavenge. The nets are now being pulled into the shore and the crowd surges in, greedy for the Pandora's Box to be opened. They must see the mystery of what the sea offers; even if it is more or less the same thing each time, there is something thrilling about catching and exposing what is normally hidden from the human eye. These are things from another environment and they carry some of the mystery of that environment with them. Not the same with hunting game that you can see on land anyway: here you do not see it until it is brought in . . . and then there is the awe of watching something live pass into death . . .

Here there is still the thrill of owning the sea. It is the last thing that is left for the poor. There are no walls and boundaries for the simple fisherman. It is moving and therefore unclaimable, and what you pluck from it is yours. You can rob, steal and plunder, for it is only your patience that you have to sacrifice, and in a poor country the sea is an endless treasure chest. The fish are like precious jewels and silver crescents and they gleam like the money that they will indeed fetch, if the catch is big enough – glistening and flickering in the sand as they are trapped by the nets, a treasure chest of bright iridescent shapes, squirming like sunlight playing over broken glass. Or diamonds. And it is not a bad catch. The large 'restaurant fish' are placed in a pile and are blindly leaping into the air or frustratedly beating their tails into the sand, and what was clean and brilliant is now dirty and sandclogged and its pearly, translucent skin becomes dull and pathetic. It seems a sad death, gasping one's life out in a squirming pile. Then the smaller fishes, as thin as playing cards and square like silver ceramic tiles, are also flickering like leaves tossed in a gust of wind. What good are these, I thought, why not toss them back? But they were thrown into a plastic bag, no doubt useful for something – maybe soup – since they were thin and fleshless. And now the nets are giving up the rest of their bounty plus the debris of this filthy sea at Acapulco, which seems to resemble a disgusting over-flowing toilet. The nets had dragged in a tangle of old, rotting refuse. There were bits of ragged toilet paper that had not disintegrated and other junk in states of semi-decomposition. Wriggling tiny fish were being unpeeled from the mess, as if the fishermen merely took for granted the polluted sea that the hideous growth of tourism had bequeathed to it. They merely prised the tiny moving bits of life from the junk as if it, too, was the bounty of the sea. Some fish were rejected outright and thrown to one side where they were now in danger of being trodden on, including one small plump fish with whiskers, which was maybe a cat fish. I watched the scrambling, naked feet and willed them not to tread on the small, live, pumping thing that was attempting to bury itself into the wet sand. Somehow I couldn't interfere with the ritual and stride out and at least throw back what was not wanted. But now the nets were being folded and I was in the way; I took the opportunity to walk over casually and pick up the little fish that had been left and, like a bored tourist, throw it back into the sea. Its little fins spun into action and it whisked off into its familiar terrain. A second one I tried to revive merely puffed for a while and turned over, too far gone to recover, but I was glad for the one that got away, which felt the sanctuary of its wet home and trusted fins to hit water and not air as it dived into the sea. Then I saw a young boy do the same. Maybe he had been watching me, and no matter how pathetic my gesture in rescuing some piece of life that was not needed, he was sufficiently influenced to do the same . . . he threw it out through the air to the receding breakers and that trip I think would not have been too healthy for it. My fish swam off and who cares about one fish, but it was a small and intricate life that man will never reproduce and it is a miracle of creation. There was also lying on the sand, a huge swollen white fish with spikes like a porcupine and distended to its utmost limit to frighten its prey, and nobody wanted it. The strongest image was all the fish that were fighting for life and slapping the beach and hurling themselves into the air, but there weren't in the end enough to fill a large suitcase. It had taken all but the best part of the morning to haul the nets in and there were at least six men to pay. I had learned what 'pulling my weight' was anyway.

□□□Beverly Hills Cop. 1984

A beautiful sunny day . . . the phone splutters into life and I crawl out of a restless night of killing mosquitoes and answer it. It is my morning call for the movie . . . *Beverly Hills Cop* . . . I am playing Victor Maitland, who is the bad guy, the nemesis for Eddie Murphy's good guy. The driver spits out a perfunctory good morning and swings the limo into the street out of the hotel courtyard, and she chews all the way to the studio her relentless swadge of gum. It makes little tacky sticking noises like a shoe walking on tar. I turn on the radio and try to drown out the tacky sound as she squeezes the gum and then opens her jaw which causes the sticky explosive smack. I catch Ravel's *Bolero* and though it helps, the noise is still there in the background. The news drones out its litany of violence and accidental shootings which are viewed by the public as auto accidents might be, seeing no causal connection between the gun and the unexpected demise of the victim. The heat is on and rising as we streak way down Venice Boulevard, where I live, and which is within the smell and sound of the Pacific pounding throughout the night. Then we slide into the muggy downtown where the smog visibly thickens and the heat increases like a pressure cooker. We hit La Brea Boulevard and then the smart svelte windows of Wilshire Boulevard. The buildings rise as the money increases, and the ground floors are all banks or exclusive shops and stores where a long black slug-like limo momentarily discharges its cargo, an ageing reconstructed face which hobbles into the stores as if they might be temples. A few people walk, but not many, and the hairdressers with salons already beginning to crowd advertise their latest blow jobs on outside video screens . . . I hope she stops the limo near the catering truck which is a giant silver trailer. I don't want to walk too far in this heat which is already beginning to do strange things to the tarmac. She doesn't stop far off, and with a 'yeah have a nice day too', I make my grateful way to the truck where the beady eye of the counter hand is already making equations on my worth in the pic. Probably thinks what an easy life compared to his . . . He's there each day at the crack of dawn and all day churning out the burgers and 'eggs over easy', while I lie in my little trailer waiting for my standby and action. Peel off a few lines, get the make-up to powder the shine off my nose and head off home with a couple of phone numbers of some nice little extras in my wallet. That's what he thinks or that's what I think he thinks . . . so let him have his fantasy . . . right now I'm hungry and the food is for free. What have you got, I ask meekly with that English reticence which years of British oppression has ingrained in me. 'What do you normally have for breakfast?' he sharply retorts, as if he will be able to throw together just any combo I like. I mustn't seem too simple, after all I am one of the stars of the movie, and as I quickly take in what one of the cops on the set is eating, I say, 'Make mine a bagel and cream cheese . . .' His face fell. He was ready to offer me the world – tamales with bacon, egg and cheese melted on top, toasted turkey with swiss and pickle – but I stuck to my bagel and cheese and helped myself from a permanent nipple of coffee that is always on the set. We don't stop mid-morning and afternoon for the teabreak, mate, here we work . . . you don't even question 30 minutes for your lunch and not an hour to piss about, fall out of character and consume large Pinewood Studios lunches . . . but the lunch here was pretty tasty and the fruit juices lay in their dozens on the beds of ice. I must confess that I feel no sense of nostalgia for the disgusting greasy spoon café at Pinewood Studios with its smell of dead fat and disinfectant.

The sun is slanting across the parking lot where the wagons containing the actors rest and where we sit in air-conditioned cells waiting for the call. Murphy's wagon is a huge trailer which contains everything that is mandatory for a superstar to have including TV, fridge, bed etc., and is always guarded by the group of heavies he surrounds himself with, as a kind of protective insulation against the prying world. They're mostly young street guys he seems to have grown up with, and he has taken the street with him rather than leave it behind. So I sit in the box and contemplate my arrival in Hollywood. I was now part of it . . . it was a swift transition from Islington to Beverly Hills and I am taking it in my stride. All the characters that I used to view on my hired video from the local shop were now here in front of me. All the locations I had seen of L.A. from the TV tube I was now part of, as if I had gone through the screen and had come out at the other side like the character in Cocteau's *Orphée* who stares at the mirror and then falls through, terrific effect. But here I was and the voices were American and resonated a little more strongly, it seemed to me, than their English counterparts. This was the cradle of movies, at least the movies that we had grown up with, and I realized how much of our consciousness of America had reached us solely through the movies. We had been indoctrinated by the power of the screen which we would queue up to see, and even before that I had been brainwashed by Captain Marvel and Superman. So here I was, playing opposite Eddie Murphy who was rising fast as America's Number One box-office hero. It didn't quite make sense, and I sat in the cooling cell staring at the lines and trying if possible to lose some of that indoctrination and view them as real, but I couldn't. The cops protecting the set with their well-cut uniforms and guns, eating bagels and cream cheese, were an image that belonged in my little screen from my rented video. So I lay there, trying not to crease my thousand-dollar suit, and ran over the lines. So he's a great comic, this Murphy, well I'll show him . . . I am not going to become fazed by all this. I wandered over to the set. The other actors greet me in their familiar American voices, which all seem so much deeper than mine and more free: I'll cope with this and take my voice down a note. 'Ready for you, Steve . . . We're just doing a line up and Martin wants you to rehearse with Eddie.' Oh God, here we go. I watch a take . . . a voice shouts 'Roll 'em!' and this sounds so much better than 'Turn over' for the camera to begin. 'Turn over' in Britain always made me feel you were just reluctant to get out of bed, but 'Roll 'em' does describe a camera's wheels turning. I stand around, trying to feel like a Beverly Hills gangster posing as an art dealer as a front for cocaine smuggling. What is an Englishman doing in Beverly Hills as a gangster posing as an art dealer and surrounded by hoods? I don't even question it. I catch a glance at myself in the window's reflection and I just look

like me, only with a reddened beach-scorched face and
heavy-looking from an overdose of tuna melts. Still I shall
act the part. I gear myself up to play the 'Bad Guy' – that's
what they call the villain out here. It's a euphemism for
every kind of criminal misdeed . . . there are no heroes
and villains, which gives a greater weight to the term and
deeper moral overtones. The bad and good implies that
both are necessary and that you got cast as the bad guy by
some unlucky throw of the dice – or lucky as it may be,
since the bad guys are the most respected as having
somehow flirted with evil or connived with the law. It's a
rebel country carved out by defiance and a healthy respect
for cheating, and so that bad guy retains a certain aura as a
rugged individualist. Viz: De Lorean who was bad guy
number one and is now worthy of a film treatment and
being canonized by Hollywood and romanticized by
James Coburn . . . it's a tough life. So I am a bad guy being
chased by current whites' black hero Murphy. OK, let's go.
I am not so nervous today since I got my first exposure the
day before in the Hollywood Hills just beneath the big
sign. The location was Bugsy Seigal's old house. I take a
shot at Eddie and he blows me away. Props man and

special effects wire me up to explode in a spray of bolognese. 'Yeah, this is a heavy gun that takes your whole stomach out.' So there will have to be explosive charges on my back so that I slither down the wall in my own claret. I ask the real cop on security, with my naïve English fascination, 'Do you shoot to kill or merely disarm?' 'Hell no,' came the immediate and fulsome reply, 'I would empty my gun.' My piteous Islington Labour Party voice queried, outraged, 'Even if he was already wounded?' – 'Sure, you never know with these guys, they could suddenly jump you.'

Somehow the sound of 'empty my gun' sounded vaguely Freudian, and expressions like 'pump him full of lead', since a pump is something that is used to discharge water and a gun is staccato and not fluid and yet the term is used to denote shooting which is also rather sexual . . . Hmmn! These and other fascinating conceptions crowded into my Hollywood-stimulated brain. 'OK, Steve, you're at the desk and Eddie comes in to ask about your friend, and you very politely dismiss him.' Eddie comes on and we rehearse a couple of times. He doesn't know his lines too well since he doesn't like them. We say hi and shake hands, and thence onwards totally avoid each other's eyes and exchange no small talk. We just get to it. How can I talk to him when he is my mortal enemy on the screen? How can I ask him how was the dancing at Carlo's and Charlie's last night and then stare coldly at him as a potential threat? So we keep away like adversaries for whom the oscillation of each other's being would only soften the edges we wish to sharpen. I sit and wait for action and fiddle with the knobs on my desk and remember which is the one to call the boys to show him out. Gotta keep cool like it is a familiar button. Action! and he comes storming in and fires off a salvo of questions and I, coolly and in the character of Victor Maitland, answer them. Cut! and we go again. Good, I got through the first scene with him and he didn't jump up and down and perform some wild act but more or less stuck to the lines. The next time he changes a few lines and gets cute while warming himself into the part. Meanwhile we hold an eyeball to eyeball confrontation. Our sequestration off camera pays off on camera. We are adversaries and do a little dance around each other, each trying to find a chink. Cut! We go again and he changes again but it doesn't seem to matter since the director obviously wants as much as he can get. I won't dry or fluff my lines even if they change for each take. That's cool, kid, come at me with all you've got. I'm getting into it and like the freedom, and am even emboldened to take one or two textual liberties myself which stopped Murphy for a split second when he adjusted with a smart riposte. Cut! We go again and this time I am enjoined not to be too 'theatrical' and the director mimes me or rather the character he saw me in from a play called *Decadence* which I took to Hollywood earlier in the year. *Decadence* went down well in L.A. and travelled well from the little Arts Theatre in damp and dreary Leicester Square to 8500 Santa Monica Boulevard, which is a decrepit end of the town and a favourite section for male streetwalkers who ply their trade to passing cars. My American acting debut . . . but still it was nice to come out on a warm night and not rush to a smelly pub and beg some surly barman to invoke the generosity of the manager and permit me a quick drink at 11pm. Here we could just go to a bar and drink and eat to our heart's content. I wonder what England has against enjoyment but it certainly seems to be involved in some conspiracy to prevent people from having too much fun, while here it is or seems a sin not to have fun. Even the catering wagon displays a sign invoking us to 'enjoy', and on the call sheet for the next week's work there is notice of a public holiday on Monday with of course the words, 'Monday free. Have fun' . . .

And you can have fun because the word 'no' has seldom graced my ears since I have been here. It's a nice sensation . . . never refused just a coffee in a café and never refused a drink in the bar. Never ordered to eat between this and that hour in a decent 'diner' which is something between a café and pub. Never difficult to get your car fixed or find a phone box, since people use them and don't have a need, based on years of 'don'ts', to wreck them or else piss in them. I believe that the closing time of eleven is not only stupid and patronizing, it actually inhibits the social life of England since most people don't like to go to a pub except in relation to another activity like going to a movie and relaxing after, or leaving a theatre at 10.30pm when the pubs crowd up in anticipation of closing. I could never see my colleagues in the bar after the show because there wouldn't be time and so we would all go home to our separate lives. Thank God for Joe Allen's in London. This is one of the first places I have actually been able to see friends and acquaintances in my profession after work. Eureka, it takes an American to create the environment. Even the beaches are havens of adventure where the full variety of the Los Angeles spirit is released in a homage to the God of Fun whoever he may be . . . nobody stops you . . . nobody to proscribe the activities of the people whose energy bursts out in one of the most amazing displays of human inventiveness it is possible to see . . . no one to say, 'No singing or busking or playing of instruments'. Here energy is released. I think that the street is the place for the natural expressions of the people on a gut level, and the forms of dance and movement are amongst the most inventive I have ever seen. The clowns perfect their act here on the boardwalk, and the kids' breakdancing is of the highest level of movement art. No cruddy disco with a couple of fat slobs on the door guarding the gates of Nirvana and permitting you entrance only after you have passed the scrutiny of their highly trained and discriminating eyes. 'Er sorry, mate. Can't let ya in like that.'

It's my call again and we are going for the 'close-ups', and this is a bore since you are off camera all but for your shoulder and you still have to remember your lines for the other actor and give them well so he can react off them. We do another half-dozen. I press the button and the goons come in and throw Eddie out – I have such power. The goons look familiar: one drives my limo and is my chief bodyguard, I seem to remember him best. Maybe I have seen him being the heavy in other movies, and now he is mine. 'OK, Steve.' He braces himself in his suit and I implore him with a significant nod to cool it and wait for me outside. Eddie comes in and out a few more times. 'Keep it cool, Steve,' the director advises. 'Roll 'em.' And I go deadly cool like a piece of ice. 'Terrific! Brilliant!' He exudes praise. He calls his first assistant to get the actors ready for the next scene and grabs a turkey sandwich in rye bread with mustard and pickle. 'Peedderr! (Peter) where are the actors . . .? Have you put a burner under their asses?' I wait around in my cell with the air-conditioning switched off and wait for the next scene and write to keep my mind off my voice and so I can come on and be fresh. Not to talk to anyone so I can just come on like a bull that has been tethered up . . . Eddie Murphy is a good actor and a fast-witted young man of twenty-three. He has a clear strong face and looks like he has tested himself in front of live audiences in the dangerous minefield of live comedy. I stare hard at Eddie Murphy and slide into my character, a smooth cool English villain. No, the bad guy.

The day's over and I'm driven home in a truck by our tough lady driver who curses every other car on the freeway. The hills of Santa Monica shimmer into view. She drops me off at Venice, where I live, a reproduction of Venice which attracted a great deal of attention half a century ago with its canals and columns and elegant hotels but which has now faded and crumbled quietly into decay. It's an early day, so I rush down and watch the sunset from the sidewalk café and the skaters are whistling past and music everywhere and the palm trees sway just ever so gently. The sun sinks down and everyone comes outside to watch. It's cooler now after being so hot an hour ago. It's crazy here on the weekends but then you can always go to Mexico.

□□□'A Little White Cloud That Cried'. Johnnie Ray. Hollywood – October 1984

Entered this club called 'The Vine Street Bar and Grill' expecting to see in the flesh someone who travelled through thirty years of time with me and came out the tunnel on the other side. What did I expect as we both crawled through the space of memory called the Fifties? I was curious to see what it had done to him. It was brilliantly cold and the steps of the London Palladium were choked with Crombie-coated teenagers like myself. My hair was curled into a soufflé of Brylcreem and the collar of my shirt rolled away like a giant wave so that any gust of wind would have had me airborne. It was in fact called a Johnnie Ray collar. It was the generosity of the collar and its creamy expanse that contrasted with the dull British two-inch collar in a desperately dreary post-war world. He came out according to memory thin and shiny and his suit glistened. His sun-coloured hair casually falling over his face. Androgynously he appealed to us all. He was male and female in an easy flow between the two, like the girl who plays principal boy in panto. It is sweet. He was hypnotic to the fourteen- and fifteen-year olds whose sexuality was still forming in the crucible of adolescence. He formed no clear image which might threaten us to emulate. He was not a heavily sexual Frank Sinatra or a greasily gross Frankie Laine or wholesome Guy Mitchell. Johnnie Ray was eerie . . . Spaced out into a world of pure emotion, his music was full of dissonances and yearning tunes. It haunted and possessed us and could even be demonic. His voice flew like an arrow directly into our emotion. It was the cry, almost a primal cry of pain. The letting out of the high tenor notes crawled into our young ears and found empathy, responding like a dog responds to the high-pitched whistle. It was intended for us alone . . . He cri . . . ee . . . iee . . . ied for us. We also yearned. We were not cuddled like our coarser older sisters by the sexual syrup of Sinatra's 'Foggy Day in London Town', to be heard in front of the fire with their spotty teenage boyfriends while they exchanged their over-fulsome gropes, and we were out in the cold. We had Johnnie Ray . . . like a winter blast. Ray was his generation's Bowie. His repetitive warbling note was a

mantra to us . . . like he was climbing a flight of stairs and reaching the top shared the view with us and then we slid down again. It was the moan or the call! I . . . if . . . your . . . or . . . swee . . . eet hear . . . art . . . se . . . ends . . . a letter of goodbyeeyyyyy. It's the pleading downbeat, the crawling for love and affection, the begging. He was begging, on our behalf . . . armed with his props to conquer the dragon that was the audience – his spear was his deaf aid and the lank blond hair falling over his eye, the thin body striking angular movements. All conspired to win us, since he was us. We were flawed and incomplete. Sinatra was already there conquering women, whereas Ray was continually *failing* and therefore like us! 'Broken Hearted Now' . . . It was not only the sanctuary he offered to our still struggling sexuality. It was as if he was beyond sex and offering up sweet and sad emotions as surrogates. The words were blatantly naive and innocent. 'Talk to her please Mr Br . . . oo . . . ook . . . speak to her Mr Rainbow and take her under your branches please Mr Tree . . . ee . . . ee . . .' Nothing sexual but even more powerful since he evoked tenderness in us. 'A little white cloud that cr . . . i . . . i . . . ied' Naïve and yet beautiful in the innocence of fairy tales or children's book illustrations . . . pastel colours and soft landscapes . . . branches of trees . . . 'Walking my baby back home, arm in arm over meadow and farm walking my baby back home . . .' While in fact we were walking in Dalston, Hackney or through the grim Orwellian council estates of Finsbury Park, where the lifts when working were used as a convenient urinal. 'We'd stop for a while, she'd give me a smile and snuggle her head to my chest' . . . The brutal gropings of early sex behind the council blocks . . . 'We'd started to pet, and that's when I get her powder all over my vest'!! Nothing more or less than the sweet image of make-up and powder. We longed for the next song.

So here I was, thrown from 1954 to 1984. I was working in Los Angeles on a movie with Eddie Murphy and my local paper advertised Johnnie Ray at the Vine Street Grill, a small bar restaurant which lay at the vital intersection of Hollywood Boulevard – who hasn't heard of Hollywood and Vine? Did I not get the same mythic longings when I was in Argos as I did when I crossed Sunset Boulevard? They stayed like ley-lines in the unconscious, bred into our memory banks in the warm cocoons of the Odeon when we were barely past walking age . . . and had we not yearned for that escapism ever since? And here I was at the centre of it. And a myth was singing, *live*! In a crummy little bar just off Hollywood Boulevard . . . Was an aged Odysseus running a tavern in Corfu? It would have felt the same . . . I heard him before I entered the club, which was a reasonably popular drinking tavern and restaurant seating about forty people with another couple of dozen in the bar. I turned up early for the second set and was shocked at hearing his voice finishing his first set on an overamplified mike. While still at the entrance of the club, the disembodied voice screeching through the speakers disturbed me enough to ask the girl at the box office to get it turned down. It was as if time and space made a sudden contraction. 'The amp's far too loud for that song,' I pleaded as if awaking from a deep hypnotic sleep. His voice overamplified and spilling out onto Vine Street had reached into the distant past and collided with my memory of him which was purer no doubt than his own of himself, since repetition had coarsened his delivery over the years and I still harboured the early pure one at the London Palladium. Untouched. A perfect reproduction lay in my head like a pristine record. Why? Because we would impersonate him, not for any desire to act but for the sheer pleasure of letting our voices go and fly as he did. I was the emissary carrying the tapes of the past. Anyway the girl agreed with me and said she would get it turned down slightly, as if any paying customer now had rights over his body and voice merely for the asking . . . so low had he sunk to be within mortal touch. I was still as concerned for him as if the last thirty years that separated us had vanished. So it was a protective emotion that he had inspired in us, and that still invoked the same loyalty as if I had at the same time been protecting the seventeen-year-old who came to watch. I wanted the image made secure, just as he was. He was after all singing the same songs. So I walked in and came face to face with my past.

He sat on a stool right on top of the audience – mostly middle-aged – wearing a three-piece suit in a dark shade which neatly disguised a reasonable corpulence, and he was beating this particular song that I remember him singing to two or three thousand at the Palladium. But then I was sitting far away. Now I could see him, close up, like going to the fringe theatre where you are always intimately near the action – so intimately at times that it takes a while to get into the play, so forcefully are the actors thrust at you with their pulsing veins and fidgety hands. And so it was with him. He sat feet away and played the London Palladium. But even so he did not disappoint me . . . I had come prepared to make quick adjustments to my old vision and so allowed for his weight and the overstressing of a song he must have played ten thousand times. It was well within the handicap I was prepared to concede. In the second set he strode on perfect . . . young-looking, radiating an innocence all the more poignant since his years had more than doubled, yet it shone through, even if he could not conceal a certain weariness. His hair was still blond-looking and fell over the side of his face, and he was still singing the memories of the past. I sat and allowed him to pull the years away from me and the other middle-aged in the audience for whom he was the touchstone of their youth. They went to the Vine and Grill to excavate a piece of their past like you might browse through old love letters, for he was not a singer that matures with age, more a photo of the past that remains the same and is taken out from time to time to disturb the memories. The picture may fade and crease slightly, but the power of its ability to evoke is undiminished. We were feeding him with our memories of him and he was merely there to remind us. Yet he had a dignity one didn't anticipate, for he sang with all his might and passion as if he had just written the damn things and ignored those unfamiliar with the legend who ate and talked through his act! His eyes scanned the empty tables, which were more plentiful for the second set, and so he concentrated on a small knot in front of him and delighted them, as if they represented the world.

I was not disappointed. The songs came rushing back like a gust of wind carrying with them indefinable clues and colours of hot and rabid teens . . . and the faces of history came into my view again. He was singing 'My Old Gal' and 'Broken Hearted Now', and nothing had changed. His repertoire had remained the same, untouched. He didn't 'cry' so much, but still was moving and took charge of the audience's emotions like a good guide taking them down Memory Lane. He still had the deaf aid and seemed unworried about revealing that he had to adjust it from time to time when his hand would sneak inside his coat and touch something situated near his heart whenever he finished a song. I suppose that when he belted he turned it down, unless he was testing that his heart was still working. Suddenly he had finished and the audience warmly responded as if we had all been present at a seance to invoke the spirits of the past. I had to tell him about 'our connection' at the London Palladium. I went backstage to his dressing-room which was shared with all the other musicians. He seemed distant as I had caught him between 'time', his place was on the stage and I had ventured to expose the mystery. He was just putting his working jacket on a hanger and I could see that he was even more comfortable than I could detect under the lights. He seemed pleased to receive my information, though I could see that everyone had a memory of him from Hoedown County to Bethnal Green. He confessed unexpectedly a slight sense of shame when I mentioned the London Palladium and said simply, 'This is an "off the wall" place to be in.' I had blundered by coming backstage and should have realized that performers would rather be seen in the bar in the safety of the atmosphere of the audience, since he made for the bar after and was visibly far more at ease there with his fans . . . I left and walked into Hollywood and Vine, the crossroads of the entertainment industry. I had taken a friend who was born after Ray 'officially' had finished, and she said, 'What an extraordinary man.' I was well and truly chuffed . . . or my seventeen-year-old self was . . .

☐☐☐Sunday, in Venice – Los Angeles, not Italy

The carnival was out yesterday. Along the strip of coast where I stay you can see on any week-end the performers of L.A. exercising every obsession imaginable to the human mind. From juggling with a live chain saw to posing as marble statues. Break dancing, my particular fave, has become more complex. Less demonic pyrotechnics on a piece of cardboard and more robotic and choreographic. Three guys work together with mind-boggling brilliance, performing split-second timing. They create waves with their arms or legs and then make them equally percussive until one would swear that motors murmured beneath their smiles. The daring and bravura would grace the London Palladium. There is a belt of smog on the ocean that looks like we are being invaded by a strange fungoid from space. I'm breathing all this in . . . although here on the beach you feel less exposed . . . It hovers out at sea like a deadly veil. There was a river of humanity on the boardwalk on this hot Sunday in Feb . . . the skaters were spinning along the blue afternoon and the crowds were watching the black skaters who occupy their own special piece of turf and dance on skates to their typically heavy sound. They sway and arabesque, wearing tiny tee-shirts exposing fulsome washboard development. Like armour plating. There is one lord of them all who dominates the whole scene and whom the crowd watch in a kind of awesome reverence . . . I am continually amazed by people out here who seem to be the real stars of L.A. and hustle for cents

on the boardwalk . . . was swept along the stream flowing in both directions . . . past endless musicians, bongo players, masseurs who will sit you down in front of the passing crowd and massage you for a couple of bucks . . . they wear white and try to look somehow like they are privy to secrets and occasionally wave a piece of crystal over your head . . . that people can allow themselves to be manipulated in public, says something to me about the sensory starvation that exists here. People seem afraid to touch each other . . . 'lovers are afraid to stroke each other's groins lest new laws against the spreading of the plague outlaw them' . . . 'Greek' . . .

Keep walking past endless lines of people queuing for endless varieties of pizza . . . $1.25 per slice . . . hot dogs, corn dogs, chilli dogs, polish dogs, giant dogs (do you remember a little stand in Leicester Square where the rotting onions stink as the now glueing mass is layered on your pale pork hot dog?), burgers, of course, in all varieties and denominations since this is the national dish and should be good . . . there is even a croissant burger since croissants are now big here, we see a photo of the once delicate French croissant being ravaged by this great greasy piece of meat wedged between it with onions, pickles and mayo. Whatever can be mixed or juxtaposed to create new and wondrous delights to create desire in the public in order to winkle the important dollar out of his purse . . . whatever you may fantasize will be made manifest in whatever size . . . I like the sizes, not just a cuppa to take out love, but in small, medium and large . . . how sensible.

So avoiding the dubious temptation of a croissant burger we drifted, my friend and I, two pieces of English flotsam placing our memories and impressions of England over the instant impression of America and they wouldn't fuse. The images would come tumbling out. One does this instinctively and automatically, contrasting what one has accustomed oneself to and what one sees. The shock can be searing and catatonic . . . you may think my God how I have wasted my whole life or you may be relieved by the contrast favouring your impression, but both sides fight with each other, each gaining ascendancy and then momentarily losing it . . . sometimes I think I am waking as if from a deep slumber as if my whole life had been in a murky cave . . . we can get used to prison if that is all we know . . .

However, England after this seems a master of restraint, caution, fear, tightness. Everything is legislated, restricted. We fear noise, dancing, singing except in places licensed for such purposes. Yes, you might get the dotty old busker in Leicester Square but anything more spontaneous will be told to move on unless as in Covent dreary Garden it is licensed . . . 'organized street theatre' . . . the very idea is a contradiction . . . we walked on past open bars in the warm afternoon, couples lingering and drinking at 4p.m., laughing and talking loudly . . . memories of the dead English villages we passed through in the summer with their beer gardens closed until 7p.m. when it was too cool to sit in them . . . past more singers and then gymnasts being
thrown in the air by one man leaping on the end of a see-saw . . . then on past the warm Pacific Ocean where surfers were making the best of too gentle waves and on past the volley ball nets (people love doing things here!) avoiding the skaters whizzing past us like angry mosquitoes, then rasping skateboards and on and on the never-ending tumble of the city that escapes to its favourite beach . . . past hot dog on a stick, past cassettes the size of suitcases, weaving one-self into an instant mood of music that hits you and then drifts off again, winding you up in its syrup before oozing away. Then we came to the Santa Monica Pier, an old crumbling Edwardian masterpiece that now was merely an extension of the boardwalk, junk food and fishermen. Here Monroe roamed in the fifties and the pier was elegant then and had a huge ballroom

for three thousand people, plus carousels and roller coasters . . . now it was a sorry shored up sight with wire netting round the base to stop whatever murky things went on beneath the rafters on those afternoons where the shadows beneath seem as midnight compared to the bright sun . . . the sun starts to sink a little and that's the sign for the thousands of cars to start forming a samba on the freeways . . . the beaches start to lose their density and the waste bins are full to exploding . . . we sit on the roof terrace and enjoy the sun creating fireworks in the sky as we imbibe a giant margarita in the Mexican restaurant . . . the sunset was as dramatic as I had seen it in the five years I have been coming here . . . it was as if a painter's easel had flattened itself against the sky and slid down . . . the margarita tasted good . . . icy and salty and plenty of tequila. We ordered nachos dipped in melted cheese and topped with guacamole, $3.50 (two pounds fifty, how bad) the evening went purple and then scarlet and indigo and at the end burst into fragments like a fiery inferno and went out . . . the tide of human energy had receded from the beach and now were jogging their heads on the freeway to their favourite tunes . . . the residents were left, the ones without homes and the bums and the loonies . . . except the majority sleeping rough are not bums or loonies . . . they are displaced people who couldn't fit in or desire to fit in . . . they pass the night in sleeping bags or when it rains, in the toilet, but tonight everyone was happy . . . the buskers made money and they always spread some around . . .

□□□New York. 8 March 1985

I slid into Manhattan day
When dawn began to shave the night
And creatures hid in coffee shops
As blue covered the world in light.

A cold stark steely blue stretched out
Bright canvas 'gainst the fire escapes,
The yellow sign of Hudson Street
The green one points the other way.

I pick up from the faces from the sounds
I gulp down life like one who's starved
And bends his legs to pick up butts,
Eyes hungry to be spared a part.

I look, I stare, my eyes are mouths
My ears are stomachs, can't get enough
I've been too long, too long starved
For the ferocity of life and heart.

I leap like a tethered starving cat
Will eat the lowest grimy scrap.
I'd suck the air from a dying corpse
If it would give my lost life back.

It is as if, as if, like lost
Like dead perhaps, outside, a ghost
Watching the bodies just steal the meat
While I, meatless, just contemplate.

No, I know, I know I didn't
Didn't I walk a thousand times
Sixth Avenue, tried to eat the past
I missed by shoving bagels in my fist.

Didn't I, yes didn't I with bulging
Eyes that clawed the skies, bite
The Chrysler in half, grabbed Hershey bars
And once yes once in a bar I laughed.

I did yes, like I do, I dipped
My toe into the ocean's brew
Then waited for the sharks to bite
And ran back to the Hovis types.

The island breathes like in one sigh
Or like some endless symphony
I, yes again the I says, throw
The drum my way, I'll keep the beat.

Of course, of course the local store
Sells everything you need, the lot, the coffee pot
Always on, the soup is hot, the bagels fresh
The coffee beans, the delicatess.

Of course, of course, it's rich, it flows
It grows, it goes on, it explodes, it never
Says no's like England's favourite sound.
Here the yes's are the streets' background.

Sunday, yes its bright cold steely blue
the plumbing barked all night and spewed
like old throats dying their last gasp
or intestines choked with old farts.

I bet she fucks up says the beast
whose mouth is foul as dragon's breath.
at 8.30a.m. she wants raw clams
and wears a dirty see-through vest.

what are they doing here at 8
fouling the morning's crisp new air
like dragging from the night their filth
and coated teeth and matted hair

their New York stomachs, goblin's homes
the ever-filled regorge as if
the world was just a smorgasbrod
they grab with two fat oily fists

beneath their raw ripped sound
their torn out chords made thick
from shouting out daily demands
french fries! too early dear, 'oh shit.'

who are these people, who and where
from whence and how? so vast and loud
such violence in their needing sound
I hear the New York underground

I hear greed whipped into a song
their plumbing spraying strings of phlegm
their fat lips trembling out the wrong
the world they think has done to them

'if a dancer wants to fuck the shit
out of a customer it's her business'
ah now the clues come streaming through
from whence these animals come, what zoo

they live to earn a buck from sex
their wombs as dead as coffin lids
their words streamlined in hate and 'shit'
that word that all occasions fit.

]□New York, June 1983.

excited I was walking down
Third Avenue from Grammercy Hotel
the air caressed the lazy crowd
that strolled through Saturday's easy swell.

the sun delivered hot, then cool
as frothy winds whipped up the clouds
a background washed in gouache blue
and diamonds spat down from high towers.

the sun shot thick bright yellow streams
and sparks flew from the clash of light
hurtling itself against the braided seams
of Chrysler's fluted satellite,

the mighty massive silver giant,
sheer heavy steel, poised like to burst
from launching pad into the pliant
sky, ripping its roots from out the earth.

so there we sat, myself and I
in ancient automat on 42
an Englishman or Ulysses
and cakes appeared in little cubes

and men with sallow faces sat
like lonely people seeking space
of cafeterias, to maybe crack
the nut of silence of their empty place.

oh yes! automatic automat
whose safe deposit boxes show
the goodies behind glass, the fat
fruit-stuffed cakes, topped with snow

the slots whose mouths have sucked
the change from billion sweaty hands
a billion quarters down their gut
a sea of coffee drowned the land.

out the great window I stared
at Chrysler's demons in frozen steel
perched on edges, obelisks to scare
the devils and the teeming swill.

damned streets, damned carnage pouring
but today the Saturday is silk
swept with cut pineapples on corners
and 75 cents a piece to eat your fill.

I wandered stretching tendons out
pump feet pound and eat the dust
hurl the photos of the past and shout
halleluya, now I wish to crush

the city to me, take it through
my veins, melt in the stream
and wrap my skin around you
and weave you in my dreams.

America was for me
an utter supreme fantasy
when I was still with sticky hands
unfolding the wonders of Batman,

the comics' thick and glossy smells
the heavy post from US aunts
to small and British suburban hell.
a child absorbed the strident blasts

of Superman and wicked vicious men
whack-zacker-splat above the skies
and Gotham City's silhouettes
and thoughts in curvy bubbles rise.

so now, yes, this is no dream
where columns glide up tall serene
majestic thousand-eyed monolith
taut tension girdled in steel mesh.

below the nineteenth century crumbles slow,
a stack of ancient houses crouch
beneath the steely towers, humbled low,
waiting for the ball of iron's punch –

and yet their ancient walls contrast
so well, a spell of memory
heat blasted years that paint
upon the face its gnarled history

below dry cleaners, express-served
and diner for your every whim
a transient and cheap hotel
and bookshop specializing in skin.

and on and yet on I walked
like a child taking his first weak steps,
head leaning back on spinal cord
to drink in dizzying perspectives.

a tramp stood still, beard grizzled white
thick slashed coat clung like shaggy mane
an animal wild in perplexed flight
caught in cross roads, dont walk, it says

he stumbles on, 'why?' etched in pain
past sunglasses made for the rich
and agony inside his brain
$200 . . . oh they suit you, miss.

and now the mouth of subway's
dark inferno in the ground
blinking as one leaves the rumbling sound
of hell that churns the night away

the long intestines soured and grim
carrying the blood of the city's life
in twisting lines of veins within
in flesh-crushed spirit worn in strife.

pick up the daily news today
let's see who's slain, whose bloody corpse
will grace the tabloid front page
some rival gang sprayed death to poor

innocent bystander who caught the slug
the freedom bullet, frontier land –
let us all have guns, you mugs,
it makes you feel the more the man!

let's look at the type/slay/anger/cops/
shoot out/fatal/mugger/rival/gang/
leader conflict/stray gunshot
a kid dies holding his mother's hand

an eight-year-old whose innocence
was smashed by men who made the slugs
whose bellies swell with bloody cents
and fat wives who practise yoga on the rug.

the counter-hand, his dishes clawed,
in one arm pours his piled up plates
like a magician making sleight of hand,
toasted cheese and salad tastes great;

he wears the uniform, black pants, white shirt
a counter hand, he stalks the aisle
hunting down orders, pencil alert –
mashed potatoes he asks, or french fried?

I walked the blazing sun-drenched streets
loved the ubiquitous and heavy air
from Grammercy Hotel I felt the heat
blast down on Third Avenue as I repaired

to morning coffee, open sheets
of news-blast – what's the treat, stared
dumbly, absorbed shock waves, death wreaked
a field day, chopped off ripe years

truck-driver killed simply by chance
as irate citizen, hating cops
sprays from sawn-off, and makes his dance
of death outside cophouse, poor Tom is snuffed,

the 25-year-old trucky who stopped
to ask directions, fated time
he found no need since time had stopped
and armaments work overtime.

more coffee please, let's turn the page.
'cold hearted tourists watched and laughed'
as Harry dived from Empire State
86 floors then splits in half

by impact said the police, they know
they shovelled up the human meat
that was the name of Harry Larkin so
his mother named the once whole piece

so once again the greatest monolith
the King Kong of Manhattan's beasts
that stands cold waiting for the breath
of victims sucked out in fatal leaps

he was the number 29
to sacrifice for Empire State
brilliant and stately, concrete and wires
sucked in its guts 10,000 brains

and chewing up their sweat and gall
its great big mouth does swallow all
then as the sun goes west in lazy crawl
it spews them out from its bloated craw.

❑ ❑Coney Island

sunday. blasted from the sky
a great round yellow melon hung
outside my window – in my eye
spun and shimmering – the day was sun

I sped to 89th in yellow car
the shimmering heat collapsed the will
of killers who sunbathed, Central Park
was filled with kosher dogs and dollar bills

hot-dogs vanished by the mile
then I was swallowed by the snake
was spat out whole with cheesy smile
as I first witnessed Brighton Beach.

I was cast out and up the stairs
when heart is light, the nimble leap
that sends quick pumps into the feet
a wide-eyed boy then hit the air

he shook off like a snake the skin
dishevelled scarred and ancient worn
in the dark subway left his sins
and leapt out strident, light, newborn

the sea-side, that's the trick, oh yes,
the cool breeze sharp tangy sea air
down old brick avenues lined with chairs
where fat old ladies speak Yiddish,

like sentinels their lazy eyes
did graze the stranger floating by
the heads stood still, the pupils spied
their ancient caution analysed,

dissected who the stranger was
striding to the well torn sea
alive escaped from the city's mob
Russian blood moved silently

a thousand heads did shake
on helter-skelter, shrieked and yelled
a million hot dogs, pizzas, baked
on open stands, the screaming sell,

'Next,' hollers loud from fat big mouth
as knishes fried and latkes flow
into the never-ending crowd
whose stomach's just one giant hole

it all poured into the vast great maw
blacks with barrel girth protect
the tiny bulge-eyed silk-skinned clawed
to papa's shoulder like limpet

the sea of sweating humanity
dancing on the toes of time
a million-headed hydra beast
and I join it by adding mine ·

become American for an hour
spend a buck and join the game
eat up the air, absorb the power
watch the muscles leap like flame

from hot black toughened teenaged rogues
treading the bikes, who fastest wins
the horse must reach the winning post
electric cracks through their steel limbs

get ready now, smash down your feet
plump wife stands by, kids on each side
you fight for them, life is complete
you won a bear, you swell their pride

casually toss the bounty fought
for kids whose dad's invincible
sometimes those lessons must be taught
certain laws young souls must feel

I soared up high upon a pole
that thrust itself into the blue
so from the top of the spinning reel
could vaguely see Manhattan's roofs

but then just pondering the squeeze
of sea and sky and Coney Isle
my dollar's power was sucked clean
and I was set down in the mire

'Next' shouts the distant shrieking mouth
the fat gut for whom man is cents.
'Next' guts to shove a thousand foul
and dead white dogs into their heads

the music swelled, the rock was loud
hips gyrated upon their shafts
they whipped a frenzy in the crowd
the whole of Coney Island danced

they danced to pounding hot rock,
teenagers wondrous of their strength
performed in solo, curled-lashed gods
sweet years before boys are men

leaping in ecstatic trance
hurled aloft the crowd-pleased eye
as one tired the others danced
like metal filings we were enticed

still tasting in our mouth the sea
we took the D train back to town
grabbing some chocolates we had to eat
the endless stations till 23rd Street

the rolling figures lolling around
being churned along the New York guts
digested by the snake, and ground
down into powder, going nuts

eyes rolling, going nowhere, sat
in sub like babes in cradle's rock
swaying like a field of wheat
waiting for the thresher's chop

'does this go to Prospect Park?'
a lolling roll-eyed head complains
I didn't know, I wanted knowledge
to ease the querying eyes of pain

we sat and ate the melting brown
and sticky bag, all sweet and full
a babe declined the offered hand
of shapeless unwanted sugary gruel

the swaying eyes stare into space
the city grasped them in its hug
of steel and iron, a hard embrace
they allow themselves to be sucked up

into the endless hole, the open jaw
the streets fly past the window pane
their dulled eyes witness familiar sores
the cracked ribs of the city's lanes.

❚ ☐ ☐Black Skater. L.A.

I saw you big black man rolling down
Venice strip/the vein of land where
skaters slide across your eyes their
sculptured hips/I saw your brutal force
packed strong like a huge mighty Rodin
sculpture in a thong/or nylon leotard
and pants/I must suppress a smile, your
elegance not wilted down, no not a bit/
by dropping your shoulder strap letting
it sway by your rib cage/your cowboy hat
white socks and boots careering softly
down/a floating capuccino in white and brown
displaying your black and narcissistic
flower in Venice town/you slid so softly
happy in your prime/like some big steak
for us to dine our eyes on/make a feast
of this black fantasy/black Samson roller
skating majesty/you would say Hi! to him/
Hallo! to her/familiar faces grin would be
demure to your huge grace/roller skating
Californian black ace/yet when I followed
your progress with English eyes/in wonder-
ment under the U.S. skies/of what more
marvels can this country show/what wealth
of fantastic and gaudy show to starved eyes
of old Europe's yellow face/the limpid dying
fast decaying race/so when this Marco Polo
journeying far like some wild errant shooting
star/did see these giants from the colonies/
these sights, these wondrous healthy Los
Angeles/he could only stare like some poor
orphan for the first time at a fair/where
everything was heaven to his hungry look/
everything was the most fantastic book of
wonders/yet in spite of all/in spite of
all this crashing display of wealth in muscle/
satin fantasy/I saw you pulling out your
shorts where they had crept up in your ass
the way they do/a little tight/they tend
to crawl right into your crack/not quite
so smart to be half up your ass/so this

small gesture multiplied so many times/your
fingers pulling shorts down to the thighs/
did make you just a popcorn king/not
mighty King Kong any more/but puffed up
swollen little boy of four/and up and down
your skates would take your mighty feet/
by end of evening when the sun went down
the mighty Samson had become a chocolate
clown.

California Morn

See how beautiful is the sky thrown across the
mountain with a trowel or like the furrowed
earth scooped and torn/or scudding across the
morning dawn like chariots of fire pierced
with the sun's bright horns/the damp earth
rained through the velvet night smells like
new bread/soft and warm/the blue stained hills
cut out in silhouette against the sky which drips
its gouache of *eau de nil* or baby blue, depending
on the light that rises over the green belly of
the sea mirrored in tearful grey and misty/some-
times like curds sometimes like whey/small pools,
torn handkerchiefs of sky fell down like flaked
plaster in the windy night and left their paint
in puddles that slowly dried returning to re-
patch the tears in the great blue tented sky/
the music oozes its confection of heart and
ache into the morning air tingeing it sweet
and colouring the sound of morning voices where
people sit and eat/golden rivers flood white
oval plates with eggs and toast and thin sliced
potato flakes/the cool fresh tangy soft light
sweet morning wind caresses my face and flits
around each jutting cliff, each precipice, round
brow and nose then curves and filters down the
cheeks, circling each nostril then sweeps and
howls around my jaw/tickles a whisper like a
spume of smoke inside my ear and pats farewell
until the next silk breath of wind appears/
cycles thinly wheel their tracks making small
cricket sounds as urgent thighs muscled like
cables of fine steel pound/their oily sweaty
pistons up and down/they gradually dissolve
into your trailing eye/sinking deeper and deeper
into the receding light/that sucks each thing
that enters it and taking little bites/and now
it smaller grows, now tiny, now a fleck/a
barely moving particle and gulp/it all flows/
it all comes and goes, 'cause now just as your
eye gave up the chase on bicycle that waved
and danced its way/and then to your chagrin

escaped/well now a dot began to grow/a spit
of colour, fuzzy, now it starts to shape and
from its globe small spikes appear, and lines
now do define that where the bike had dis-
appeared into the hungry lion, it vomited back
into your eye a moving piece of life/I turned
my eye away onto my golden plate which then
appeared/my eggs all warm did flow and like
pure molten lava glowed/or as L.A.'s giant
rolling hills, the eggs did o'er the snow
white plate tumble and spill/the ketchup in
its bottle gleamed all bright rich ruby red/
I gripped, twisted its metal cap, poured
out its saucy blood/it plunked, globbed down
and splashed the egg which now wounded did

seem/as fork and knife slashed, dug and cut
and scooped my breakfast feast/ooh crumble
smear the golden rye with thick rich drooling
beurre/and gather eggy nuggets on the toast
so there/would be a crush of tastes swilling
round my tongue/while in my other hand I
grabbed a cup of coffee, poured it down/the
dot that now appeared waving and bobbing
growing larger by each stride/expanding in
the centre of my eye/it now was filling up
the space/now growing larger with each pace/
a runner eating up the air, advancing/soon
it will appear with puff and pound/his head
and chest now leaping up and down and left
and right as if the earth shook him from
side to side/he lacked the grace of sinewed
muscle in its holy state obeying rhymes so
intricate to make a body seem to float in
space/but like a puppet dangling from its
strings/held by a drunken master so it
seemed/he thrust his head this way and that
as if his nerves and muscle were at war/each
struggling to obey a different drum/his limbs
threshed, struck the ground beneath his
withered steps which sent shocks to his trunks
which spun away/as if a mighty fist had punched
and made him sway, just then this body sculptured from his waist of rippling embroidery of
muscle to his face so etched in pain/I then
saw the reason for his ungainly shape when on
two crutches he attempts his tortured race/
his bravery did move us all/our knives and
forks stood still/our hearts moved more/his
withered limbs so shrunk were as two twigs,
his feet dragged just as if . . . no feeling
flooded through those useless legs/and all
his might did rest on those two wooden pegs/
which hit the hard cement and pushed him
through/then once again he lifted up his oars,
dragged up to sink once more into his daily
hard routine/to run like any other human, keep

his dignity in jerky ugly jog/but now to me/
it was his soul that flared from out his pain/
his early morning tryst, his tortured face/
because this poor valiant man ignored the un-
fair stroke that shattered what we have/so
naturally to be blessed with sympathy of muscle,
brain and nerve/to move each separate digit to
the inspiration like a bird/I saw him dance
away into the distant swarm/his hopping gait/
his grimace filled my eye/and warned us all
who once again stuffed mouths with eggs and
coffee and gain/of the frustration that we
do ourselves complain/that here was love that
overcame/the desperate misfortune and hurt
and turns it into blinding inspiration that
must burn/into our self satisfied and greedy
smirk.

## The Plague, U.S.A.

If the smog don't get you in its grip
With its deadly carbon monoxide mix
Then Aids will wait until you're ripe
Then chew your corpuscles with deadly bite.

We'll get you in the end, no fear.
We'll hurl a billion cancer cells
Gift-wrapped in a million chemicals
To make the food you eat look swell.

You avoid the junk and read the text?
No colours, no preservative,
You eat organic, no meat, no fat.
You drink wheat grass and meditate?

We'll get you yet, we'll cut you down.
Radiation is still around.
How many nuclear bombs were shit
By an asshole in the White House john?

While you eat your bran and figs
And jog in the polluted fumes
And fuck now with transparent tubes
And suck each day your vitamins

And do aerobics till you faint
And get a waistline like a wasp
Eat fibre to make turd-like cigars
And carrot juice to make you fart

A bigger explosion now takes place
Beneath the desert way down deep,
Atomic fusion tears apart
The earth while you can soundly sleep.

The earth shudders, groans and aches
It's live, organic, gives sweet air
Its juices feed our bones and sap,
Mr President drops his pants and craps..

Just like a dog digs in the earth
To cover up his smelly shit
At least the soil will drain the best
But what's it doing with Reagan's filth?

I'll tell you, wanna know, old boy?
It creeps into the broken rock
What seeks a way will find a way
A little rainfall finds a crack.

The water travels through like blood,
Like blood will join the arteries
The arteries the nerves and veins
One day you'll wake up with a pain.

'Sorry there's a shadow on your X-ray'
Oh God I don't smoke, drink, or screw
Don't eat meat, and buy health foods
Meditate and do yoga too!

'Sorry, I'm sorry, you have Medicare?'
Yeah sure, what can I do, please tell
I'll do anything, what regime
To make my body sweet and clean?

If Aids doesn't get you, fleeing man,
And plants a serpent in your brain
And radiation just misses your house
Like God passing over the Israelite slaves,

And carbon, chemicals, DDT
Deadly fish from polluted streams
Giant industries killing bees
And acid rain that skins the trees,

We'll get you, we'll get you, we will,
We'll arm an army of discontents
Brains blasted by bullets on TV,
Wealth sex power that he'll never see –

Gimme! gimme! I wannit, wannit all
How to be rich, be rich, make more.
How to make money, make money, make it
There's only shame in being poor.

You can't be too thin or too rich
Look at your cousin in Bangladesh
Is she too thin, is he too rich
Aah? Don't tell me, let me guess.

We'll use your greed and hate
We'll make you our new Frankenstein
Programmed by junk heroes on the screen,
His new commandments, 'Gimme! gimme!'

One day you'll come awake in pain.
A microbe stole inside your vaults
The safe wherein you store your seed
It loves to attack you in your balls.

I'll buy a gun, it's easy here
Where you can buy just anything
Dollars sanctify the act
Of selling guns to lunatics.

I'll get you boy, one night alone
I'll break inside your home sweet home,
I'll kill you dead, hate rules me boy,
Mothers, daughters, children, fly!

Hate, rape, attack, assault
Stab, shoot, burn, smash,
Armed response, guard dogs, guns
Can't stop me when I'm having fun.

I'm a microbe of self-destruct.
It happens when you hurt the earth
Hurt people, then life will react
It seeks to destroy the ugly fact.

Ban the Bomb . . . OK . . . OK
It's just a symbol of the malaise
It's only a link in the deadly chain
Of self-interest and 'We'll do it my way'.

Then ban the gun and ban the greed
Ban the need to spend your bucks
By sticking your profits up your nose
Each snort will feed ten empty guts.

Then ban next the garbage TV
That unloads on the collective head
The 'messages', a deadly word
To describe the sewers' deadly turds

It flickers day and night death rays
To penetrate inside your cells
To make your brain a catacomb
And there the rats will incubate.

We'll get you in the end, don't run
There's no escape, no credit cards
Will help you when you drop the bomb
To preserve Disneyland and Dynasty.

□□□19 March 1985. Los Angeles

I ate in Cantor's delicatessen
where pickles leap into your eye
and beef is sliced up to the sky
24 hours a day in rye

the broken dolls of waitresses
whose fluffy blonde hair tops a face
that's weathered miles of pounding feet
beneath the ageing carapace

dressed in white, the uniform
for delis dealing in dead meat
meat that's salted, stewed or fried
barbecued but piled mile high

meat sliced fine on steel machines
meat wobbling on trolleys, steam
meat that's gorged, chewed, swallowed whole
glued in mustard, pickles and dough

the fat, obese, obscene crawl in
the temples of the overweight
the altar where you purge the sin
of hunger and stuff till you faint

oh Bangladesh, oh Ethiope,
oh, Delhi, Culcutta, Sudan
oh babies' arms thin as the ropes
that stop the diners pouring in

oh swollen stomach filled with air
oh eyes clawing the empty air
oh hands grabbing snatching on air
oh god, where? somewhere out there

let's make a sweet pop song or tune
let's pour some love and dollars too
and then we'll buy some grain and fuel
and then sleep well in Malibu.

corned beef on rye, pastrami, lox
a reubens, cheese melting on top
the beef sliding over the edge
torn out entrails called sweet breads

heart lungs liver, kidneys too
balls and brain, a witches' stew
throw in a toad or hangedman's grease,
hey, I'll have that on sour dough please!

24 hours it daily churns
could fill a half of Africa
with what it puts between two buns
now open wide and down it slurps

oh precious Cantors, holy deli.
not Delhi, India, home of saints
but deli home of gefilte fish
fat matzo balls and stomach aches

the paradox, don't question it
the tv brings you starving babes
watch Dynasty or dried up tits
that starving mouths will suck in vain

the tv brings into your home
the suffering of the human race
if you could now reverse the tube
and send corned beef on rye through space

who are we to feel some guilt?
we worked, we paid our taxes, rates
we paid for our trailer home
that we use on . . . sunny days.

did Jesus say 'listen my brethren
it is easier for a camel to go
through the eye of a needle
than a rich man go to heaven?

do you want heaven? no, 'course not!
you don't believe in all that shit
I pay my taxes and keep the state
religion's for the old and kids

what will you do with all your wealth?
invest it, man, in outer space
since there ain't no god out there,
stake your claim before the race.

did Jesus say give up your wealth?
I pay my taxes and my rates
but when I die I must confess
I ate far too much (burp) delicatess.

❏ ◻Marcia A. Timmel

the air is fresh and clear today
a lone wind surfer slides the sea
a plane drones over marina del rey
the palm trees sway just so gently

the breakfast sits and integrates
the menu's large as Genesis
I had to choose, the waitress waits
french toast and coffee, decaf please

the *l.a. times* regurgitates
the agony of los angeles
the drugs, the crime, the nuclear waste
marcia a timmel wrote a piece.

she tried to hammer a submarine
the Trident into a great ploughshare
her protest made a little scratch
upon the nose of a raging bear

the bomb envelops everyone
the nuclear shadow grows so long
like father walking by your side
'it will protect you, little one.'

beneath the surfer with red sail
slicing the blue into twin tails
beneath the green heads of the palms
beneath the golden sun and tawny arms

beneath the flickering sun-licked waves
beneath the migrating grey whales
heading to california to mate
beneath the dolphins' escapades

the Trident moves like deadly turd
bulging in pain to defecate
unloose its bilious choked up guts
that has on it ron reagans name

by proxy we live through the games.
our weakened phallus, hawker jets
our impotence an m60
our constipation . . . submarines

our lack of vision, satellites
lack of belief, spy planes on high
lack of balls, mx missiles
our lack of love, christ crucified.

our lack of strength, a nuclear house
no window of vulnerability
no danger of a little air
on geriatric lying there

block up the window, there's a crack
senile feeble voice raps out
bang in a missile when it flaps
a few more war-heads'll make it stout.

put out the light and go to sleep
you sure you locked the nuclear gates?
can you see anything? no, not a peep
ah! now we're ready to negotiate.

☐☐March 24, Los Angeles – Peter Patowski

I saw peter patowski, clown,
street comic, sometime in white face?
follow people and mime unknown
to the innocent dupe, their personal traits

we'd stand around and hoot and grin
while he'd trail some poor man or child
follow their step in unison
but his cruel mock would drive us wild

or else whip out red plastic lips
a passing black guy turns and glares
but laughs at the grotesque comic's wit
the crowd all watching applaud the dare

or else fat mum with child strolls past
so unaware of conflict zone,
she enters; clown like spider darts
and grabs her arm like neglected son

now he pretends to be lost child
while other real one, real confused
so unaware of street clown wit
he never learned that stuff at school

the crowd goes past, he looks for bait
in which to fasten his cruel hook
and dangle his catch on a plate
for us to ogle, stare and taste

we like the taste of human blood
as long as we are spectators
not victims, not to be the cud
he chews and be spat out again

peter patowski's cartoon lips
stretch like pancakes, balloon cheeks.
this is, he says, his farewell quip
dizzy gillespie when he sleeps.

beneath the glaze of usa
yes, the beneath the surface paint
what russian or rumanian stew
put blood in this comedic saint?

this is he says where belushi
coke stuffed and laced with H imbibed
the hotel on the sunset strip
his comic's heart lay down and died

poor belushi, the fat man clown
force-fed with bucks to make us laugh
go pull a face and tell a joke
500 faces want ha ha.

fat belushi, thick greased in fame
slop gutted, coke pissed in drains
blade blunted, his comic's knife
the heads don't roll, they're tickled instead

## March 27

It's rain today on venice shores
fine drizzle softly licks the air
I woke up and the day was grey
I thought of breakfast as I walked

a throng of kisses on my head
so unfamiliar rivers formed
within the shrubland of my hair
and down my brow poured waterfalls

I squelched across the old boardwalk
deserted as a new born day
just one runner jogs and smiles
beneath the ashen clouds, then fades.

but the air like gulps of wine
pure quaffs of rainwashed oxygen
soft as shadows, sweet as pine
I greedily inhale it in

□□□

I like the slow dead afternoons
that seep into the venice streets
like butter slowly pouring through
and lazy cats lick up the heat

the shutters, worn out wooden frames
paint peeled and bike on porch
signs, don't park and oily stains
beneath an ancient rusting ford.

beneath the even taut blue sky
whipped with white furry tails
and burger and avocado mixed
fruit shakes and dripping tuna melts

I know, I know it's fun to chase
the sun from coast to coast
sensation every time I taste
california between rye toast

I know that's not all, not a jot
of why I love to live and be
pounding the boardwalk after dawn
between sun, sand and endless sea.

☐ ☐Hollywood Movie

Waiting-waiting-waiting around.
The sun pours down, then drifts away
The shadows lengthen on the ground
And eat into another day . . .

'OK, let's go!' The figures move.
'Ready!' a voice calls from the gloom.
A clapper snaps, the cameras roll,
On 'Action!' actors clear their throats.

'Quiet please . . . rehearsal!' someone yells
It all goes quiet, just the birds
Who sing and twitter in the hills
And pine trees release their summer smells.

A stuntman sits and talks of feats
To a fellow crony, and just nods
Fights are not what they used to be,
Not when you had the Duke and Steve,

This used to be Bugs Seigal's house
The walled surround, the pool on top,
The tiled fountain and terra cotta
The view that makes you gasp out, 'Wow!

Wow! what a place!' The valley spreads
Beneath your eyes . . . a paradise
The Hollywood sign sits up high
So all the world will raise its eyes.

The sunburnt valleys, green and mauve
The cypress trees indent the hills
The mansions stand remote alone . . .
Beneath, Hollywood freeway spills . . .

Then in the blinking waning sun
The sky is bluish red and scarlet pink
The dry gorse glows as evening comes
And lizards slink within the weeds.

'Action!' he calls, and 'Raise your gun!'
A Magnum 60 the model reads . . .
'Now smile just as you use your thumb'
To cock the trigger's deadly C.

'Just smile and raise your arm real slow'
'Is this OK?' the actor pleads.
He checks the image in the hole
Where dollars manufacture dreams.

'It's great, it looks real good,' he says.
The blast echoes throughout the house
I raised the gun after the blaze
Just like the way I was advised.

This was my first. My Hollywood.
The first time I invaded time
To place myself within the wood
Where holly is a white-teethed smile.

My suit's prepared, my tie is slick
I raise the gun again, real sly
My first exposure on the print
A gun against an empty sky.

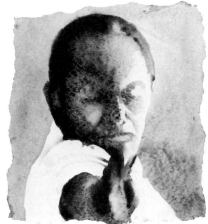

This is how you view the world
You grab a bacon bagel first,
The sun sweeps down and swipes your neck
You wait until your name is heard . . .

'OK, action! no talking please!'
This is the shot, his POV.
The body in the bathroom bleeds
The flies invade the lemon trees.

'The scene today is your death fall.'
Your shirt is rigged with sacks of blood
That will on action spout their gore
While you pretend the bullets thud.

The Star is introduced to you
He surfaces from out his cave
The giant trailer where he plays
His tapes and keeps from public view.

'Hi! and how's it goin'?' is the code
The handshake and the teeth exposed
He stubs your face out in his head
The moment you have turned the bend.

The sun sinks down while L.A.'s rise
The jewelled crown now spikes the sky
The cameraman says, 'Two more shots
Before the light begins to die.'

It's over now, the field explodes
With cars that are keen to get home
It's called a wrap, my debut done
I fired a really heavy gun.

Day Two

We wait and wait and wait and wait
I sit in some small wretched box
The air conditioner's fan now grates
And shit clogs up the toilet bowl.

It's hot as hell, and managers
Will come to see their clients play
Their role and hear the lines they say,
'And will this make a lot of dough?'

'Yeah, that grossed twenty million bucks
The first six weeks or so it ran
The Hollywood movies now suck,'
Says the smart dark-glassed studio man.

The scene when you shot so-and-so
Is just so fabulous, so great
When you got shot, my God
The blood oozed out like marmalade

'The scene with you, with her, with him' –
The nice director's daily hymn
To help this actor's nerve and mind
Were great, were simply great. He's kind

'Should I get up?' You're super cool
You don't move, not an eyelid tells
The turmoil in your heart and soul
The chilliest villain in the world.

You don your 1000 dollar suit
That looks like it cost 50 bucks
Do up the shirt from Bond Street too
And put the fake gold in the cuffs

Oh gosh it's fucking hot today
The hours chew my mind away
The nagging thoughts chew up my peace
'Cause brain sits like a dead carcass

And flies feed on a still dead thing
I write to keep away their stings
I think to keep the brain alive
I live to act but then I die,

And when I see my life
Drift past like newspapers in drains
That choke up and disintegrate
As it tears slowly in the rain

And so this space, this wait, this loo
Choked up, it smells just like a zoo
The fan that chills the deadly air
And stare in mirror, comb your hair

'On set please!' Pulse begins to pace
The whole day geared to this one stunt,
To make yourself as cool as ice
Not tense, stiff, nervous, choked up runt

If only I was Hamlet or Macbeth
Or even Faust would do, or play
A part that grew, the more you fed
Into the camera's guts your face,

Then you would be so calm, relaxed,
The voice stretched out, the body loose
Not coming for a second's snatched
Before you've time to make the cool.

But no, you must appear each time
Like you've been waiting primed to flow
Not sweating in anticipation brine
For the one moment when you hear 'Let's go!'

⬛Hell in L.A.

oh god, oh god, oh god, oh god,
forbid the streets, forbid the streets, forbid.
the heat, the heat, the overwhelming heat, the heat.
Devouring me, devouring me, devouring me,
my feet my feet my aching feet, my aching
bruised and battered feet, the concrete concrete
smashing flesh and bone and blood, wasting me,
wasting me, eating toes and heels and ankles,
calf and knees, groin, sinews pounding pounding
left and right, right and left. walk relentless
straightened murdered streets, the murderers
of meat and heart and lungs. the asphalt blasting
mix of heat and street and siren shriek,
oh god, oh god, forbid the monster snakes,
the freeways, deathways crushing twisting me,
a roller coaster's death highways.
slabs and slabs of metal glass and brakes.
instructions stab the neon sky, where to take
your piece of suffocating ache, which intestine
to suck you down, grind jerk and break.
a million million faces strange grip wheels
in sweaty hatred haste. mother fucker out of my way!
the mind's computers etch their scroll of agony
upon the human race. oh god oh god oh god oh god.
dont walk. walk. dont walk. walk. dont walk. walk.
run escape, heart – beats accelerating ache,
pressure cooker, heat and monster obelisks
temple silos rising greet the smoke stained
filthy sun that burns the carbon sucked into
my hurting lungs. run and run the street becomes
conveyor belt that rats run on. tread mill
the more you race it follows on. the faster
faster it will follow you relentless shadow
killing you, stalking killer sucking you,
your blood by drop by bloody drop.
oh god help me help me oh help. he cant
see me beneath the stinking monoxide pelt.
a dot moving down in hell, a snail leaving
its spore among the city's horrid swell.

☐☐☐Farewell Venice (U.S.A.)

and will I learn to say farewell
to this fair land/the sirens
wow wow wowing/hurtling down the strand
the cop's light twisting its tormented globe
a beacon spinning like an angry red
all seeing eye/its light and sound
compound to make the guilty shake

or when slow death defying slumber
crawls inside my brain to numb
the day and soak the pain away
when suddenly I dreamed a giant moth
against deceptive pane did flap
seeking the light with deadly cracks
but then my ears did read the flack

a chopper's wings sliced through my peaceful sleep
a cutting edge severed the misty form
a helicopter slashed the air and scored
a hamburger it made of all my thoughts
a cursed cracking by its spinning blades
a tangle of the webs of night it made
a man did toss and turn seeking the day

I grabbed the thin white cotton sheets' membrane
as if to cover up the wound of human pain
as if within dark worlds the sheet would cure
as if wake up brand new again and just
for once be clear bright eyed and pure
I tossed and turned and waves they heaved and fell
mosquitoes buzzed all night/I dreamed of hell

and then seeking within the cushion's cheek a space
seeking to form a soft egg shell, my face
did comfort itself against the cool and soft
white pillow that was like the mother's breast
which closed itself against my burning cheek
and rocked me into certain childlike sleep
mosquitoes drank my undiluted me!

and then the dawn crawled up the ocean's back
and perched, red tousled hair, became the sky
a fleeing cloud shaped holes for two pink eyes
and then hot gold did pour between the cracks
the ocean wind became the morning breath
the sea, a thousand white tongued beast
or heaving mother giving cubs her teats

I crawled from out the sulky sweaty night
like butterflies so pleased and free from jail
the cocoon where I spun oneiric wings
that were the dreams I made in vain
I stretched my trembling arms and viewed my blades
that now did sprout like abalone shells
and fluttered both and floated on the day

the sea was yet deep and blue as eyes
of puking kittens newly strewed
and wavelets bobbed and bounced upon the shore
like puppies fetching ball and back for more
and shadows crawled across the sunburnt rocks
as slow as snakes just woken up
the sand was yellow as a buttercup

oh yes, get up, film time, a cup of tea
boiled water and a bag attached by string
the early morning chorus of dumb yells
that from the jungle that is venice beach
those things that slept outside unfold and screech
the garbage truck collects and burps the junk
that's forced into its guts and sweeps

oh ho, so this is venice, no not italy
not gondolas swift cutting green canals
nor statues carved by masters renaissance
nor cathedrals dripping with Christ's face
nor ancient timbered buildings and old lace
nor history that's layered in the air
and when you breathe it you smell Dante's hair

here what you breathe is toms café
hamburgers 24 hours a day
an alley where the bums do piss
a giant dustbin for the thrown out waste
and groaning faces blasted not in stone
but from the years of freedom u.s.a.
that have chewed their poor lives away

here come the bleeding and old
here come the young bums broken from their homes
here come the alcoholic stewed brains
here come the junkies crawling out of drains
here comes the poor black and his bride
his fist clutching dollar forty five
that he needs for cheeseburger and french fries

round tom's café, hamburger and hot dogs
the stink of recent urine and the squelch
of rotting scraps, small piece of hell
inside the game machine makes vicious sounds
while rapping out symbolically death knells
destroying your opponent on a screen
since murder makes your heart feel good and clean

□□□The Faces Stare

the faces stare out meekly from tom gloom
slurp down their breakfast to their tunes
clutching their tin cassette decks like a bride
that will, no never them deny . . .
will play the sweet sounds yet just once again
they hold them like a dear sweet friend
the smells waft up like from the dead

turn now face forward, face the sea
not back . . . not back inside the l.a. scene
where broken backs of houses stake their claims
don't dare to park, don't trespass, hints of pain
turn now to face the crispy light blue sky
let the joy of life pour in your eye
run run run pound feet and thigh

the sand and quiet early new dawn day
as yet so unpolluted like a flower
not yet picked nor exposed or claimed
no not yet trodden on or stained . . .
just calmly taken like a morning stroll
heart pounding and the day pours into you
the sun and sky and air are whole.

and now the forlorn gathering up
to sell the car or not, to sell or not
no let it stay while you go back to earth
let it be waiting for your swift return
you tie up all the ends and view the world
this is the place that you did once unfurl
this was your home, on this earth's plot.

you cut and dug and sent shoots bursting through
you ripped the clay and in it dipped your toe
you pierced the fruit of the u.s.a. tree
you said want part of you be part of me
you needed to uproot your ancient past
you pulled the roots white-knuckled oh so fast
you then decided, maybe home at last

what made you such a sinner in your thrust
what curse put boomerangs in wanderlust
what makes us say when time is time
what, have you drunk enough the wine?
what merely sipped the nectar of the gods
what? rushing back to safe familiar sod
what makes you turn again you worm

yes, it's true . . . the blood boils . . . the eye can see
yes, the heart whimpers for you and thee,
yes, the sun's bright, the faces strong.
yes, the new world breaks our old song.
yes, cut the umbilical to mother earth
yes, free yourself, arise in your rebirth
yes, quivering, new the soul at last breaks through.

dont live once more to say, if only I
dont ever do nothing and then say . . . why?
dont let a dream slip by and let it fade
dont let your arms hang dumbly like dead weights
dont fail to grab it with both hungry hands
dont fail to notice the celestial plan
dont dream it. *Shit* go for it man!

□□□Roller Skater

I saw the mister mad/the sun just poured
its streams of blessed honey on the scene/
he roller skated, teeth and tongue uproared/
not weekend just a wednesday eve/
dancing his marble sculpture gorged in blood/
each cut chipped out by angelo
he could have been his model even so

did you ever see joy so manifest
did ever laughter sound the devils horn
did alabaster or stone get so caressed
did you see statuary have such form
did you see mister mad make pirouettes
did you? rolling on steel wheels to tunes
did the sun set and introduce the moon

⌐☐ ☐On the Wrecking of the Santa Monica Pier by Storm, 1983

The pier was smashed last night/
The storm chewed through and ate
The wood that held the rafters/
Held the mood of lingering smells
Of summer and the spell of sunsets
That so slowly fell while you on elbows
Cupped your face and leaned against
The old pier's washed out frame/
The crest, the crown, the head
Was chopped just where you leaned
And lines were spent in hope/
Of hooking from the deep a living
Fishy thing/a storm sent crashing
Tons of seething beating fists and
Smashed the old and aching timber/
Shuddered cracked and groaned
Heaved split leaned over dragging
Down the dreams/the buckling and
Split seams and knelt like old
Boxer stunned from pounding blows/
And then like slow, it shuddered
Sank and died into the deep and cold/
And waves buried the old and shaggy
Head/its warm and sun drenched planks
Where all the hopeful feet did stomp
And stamp/the wives with tattooes
Threw their lines with cruel hooks
And husbands squint their eyes
And coffees drunk and DJs squeal
Their stuff from steel cassettes
And kids would scream and shells
Were cracked for things to use as
Bait, the stink of dead and fishy
Slimed the deck and lazy talk would
Float into the blue and hazy hue
Mixed up with saccharine old songs
Which wooed the throng who cracked
The afternoon with coffee, hamburger
And cool silk breezes lifted skirts

And guts, beer swelled hang over belts
And I drank coffee with a tuna melt.

☐☐☐

And watched the sun-split seas
Wrote poetry and felt the blood
Begin to rise when a line of mine
Did hook a rhyme and up it flew
All wet and flapping coloured in
Hues from fathoms deep and scrawled
Its sleek and new born soul in
Words across my page and shoals
More sweet did tumble in my net
I crushed my teeth into the tuna
Melt where Japanese or Viet did
Fry the breakfast for old guys/
With hats and peaks and old ladies
Said 'more coffee, sure'/I gripped
My pen/ate up the hills and tore
The seas into salt lakes
That formed small pearls
In corners of my eye when
Sky and sea poured endlessly
And ate the fish and drank
The coffee and said thankyou
You're welcome came the swift
Reply/and ventured out where
Sky stretched clouts of puffy
Cloud and mounds of flesh leaned
Smoked and waited for the sea
To leap in shape of wiggly salty
Things/and then at bloody end
When sun dripped iron in the sea
And made a blood red fantasy
And folks thinned out and giant
Pelicans did scout for flesh
Thrown up by kids who loved the
Jaws that snapped and trapped a
Sardine or thing too small to take
Then one dark raging night giant
Waves did curl their mitts and

Fought the ageing trembling legs
That gave up sagging no blame
Can be attached or stain can
Blemish its old head where poems
And fresh fish did fly and birds
Cut shadows from the sky and old
Men leaned against your thighs
And children cried and I, yes I
Would ask for tuna melt/and when
You died old pier I, yes I, let
Out one huge and heavy sigh.